"[T]he vandals who are now waiting to enter into this wonder-land, will in a single season despoil, beyond recovery, these remarkable curiosities, which have required all the cunning skill of nature thousands of years to prepare."

Ferdinand V. Hayden, 1871

"Hey, did y'all see the nice things Ferdinand V. Hayden said about me?"

Yellowstone Rob, 2024

Fraud: The Art of the Steal

Satirical Lessons from the Trial of Donald J. T—

Yellowstone Rob

Cryptoversal Books

Contents

Publisher's Foreword

by Cryptoversal

This past summer, Cryptoversal Books put out a tech-progressive call for manuscript submissions. We issued a collection of NFTs that gated access to our decentralized submissions app, and the query letters poured in. We received proposals from hundreds of talented authors, but none sparked the interest of Sylvie, our submissions editor.

At around the same time, a sheaf of papers arrived the old-fashioned way: over the transom, through a window, wrapped around a brick.

The manuscript arrived in chunks, out of order, scrawled in red marker on pages that smelled like the wilderness, with not a single Oxford comma in sight. The staff and I dismissed the manuscript as yet another screed from yet another madman, but this madman would prove more persistent than most, and our office ran out of windows before he ran through his supply of paper-wrapped bricks.

I had our communications director arrange a meeting with the author, a Mr. Yellowstone Rob, at a local diner. Yellowstone Rob presented himself as an eccentric real estate developer with an unbelievable resume—literally unbelievable, in that he claimed to have amassed more personal wealth than Elon Musk, Jeff Bezos, and Mark Zuckerberg combined using a proprietary system in which his assets remained entirely theoretical.

Before we got down to business, Yellowstone Rob finished off three plates of corned beef hash (no salt), a half-dozen soft-boiled eggs (no toast), and a carafe of black coffee (no sugar). After wiping the drippy yolks from his face with the cuff of his brown suit jacket, he pitched me his project: a manual on how to do frauds.

I raised an eyebrow. "Are you experienced in the topic?"

"Experienced? Hah! Yellowstone Rob has studied the best of the best." From inside his jacket, Yellowstone Rob produced a black paperback so worn down by the fingers of time that the gold letters of its author's name could only be read as "Donald J. T—." A co-author's name had been obliterated, possibly by malice or possibly as a mercy.

"I'm familiar with this book." I picked up the paperback and looked into the eyes of its famous author's portrait. "Are you suggesting this business biography as a market comparable to your own book...on fraud?"

"T—'s book is full of words, Yellowstone Rob's book is full of words, they're both full of words, so of course they're comparable."

"But are your words any good?" I prompted.

"Pfff," he spat. "That old master of the grift would tell you he has all the best words but really, he just has the loudest voice. Meaning doesn't matter as long as the message spews out with the force of a firehose. But words are cheap, especially when filtered through a lack of self-awareness. Actions have the potential to be so, so, sooooo much more valuable. Yellowstone Rob is a scholar of those actions. Yellowstone Rob is a student of the Sixteen Frauds of Donald T—, which he has personally applied to become—"

Yellowstone Rob stood with one foot on the booth and the other on the table. He raised his arms for dramatic effect, causing five stolen settings of cutlery to spill out of his sleeves and clatter against the ceramic floor tiles.

"—The Wealthiest Person in Human History (On Paper)™!"

He held his pose, surrounded by pilfered silverware, bits of egg still dripping from his left ear, and with a clear expectation of applause, praise, and a lucrative publishing contract. Other diners around us cringed and shook their heads before returning to their pancakes and coffees.

I continued chewing my Western omelette. Eventually, Yellowstone Rob returned to his seat. Having finished his own meal, he pulled my half-finished plate across the table and dug in. I'd lost my appetite anyway. "Are you worried that this book of fraud, based on this particular subject, might be seen as politically motivated?" I asked.

"Political? Oh, Yellowstone Rob stays out of politics. Let the parties battle, let them fly their blue and red banners, let them promote one side's stuffed suit over the other side's stuffed suit. Yellowstone Rob doesn't have a dog in the fight or a team on the field. Yellowstone Rob is all about business, y'see, and only business. Why? Is there something political about this old book on making deals?"

"You're telling me that you don't follow presidential politics? That you honestly don't know or care who the President of the United States is or was?"

"Honestly," said Yellowstone Rob. "As honest of my claim of being The Wealthiest Person in Human History (On Paper)™."

"And why do you think Cryptoversal Books is the best publisher for your book on fraud?"

Yellowstone Rob blinked at me as if I'd said something amazingly obtuse. "You publish NFT editions of your books, don't you?"

I dropped some bills to cover the check and strode to the exit. At the door, I turned back to issue a parting shot. "Yellowstone Rob, no publisher would ever stake their reputation to platform your tribute to graft and thievery."

I thought that would be the last I'd ever see of Yellowstone Rob, but I was wrong.

Dead wrong.

Continued in Publisher's Interlude #1...

The Sixteen Frauds

#1: Claim to Own Everything

#2: Manifest a World without Limits (or Laws)

#3: Things Are Worth Whatever You Say

#4: Options Are Just Pre-Broken Promises

#5: If You Can Dream It, You Can Earn It

#6: Think Inside the Box

#7: Keep the Best Part for Yourself

#8: Everything is Comparable to Everything Else

Meet Yellowstone Rob

The Wealthiest Person in Human History (On Paper)™

The Deal of the Art

Yellowstone Rob once read a book about art, or deals, or *The Deal of the Art*, or somesuch. It made a big impact on him at the time, and he carries a copy around as a lucky talisman. But this long, bestselling, cleverly ghostwritten business bio wasn't the catalyst that transformed Yellowstone Rob into the (On Paper)™ real estate tycoon he presents himself as today.

In Yellowstone Rob's opinion, *The Deal of the Art* exists mainly to aggrandize its subject. Instead of enriching readers, the book instantly drops the luckier ones into an $18 financial hole while its hardcover patrons must struggle to find $30 of value within those same pages.

Yellowstone Rob's main takeaway from *The Deal of the Art* was that Yellowstone Rob would need a library card to read *The Deal of the Art*.

Once the borrowed book was conveniently "lost," Yellowstone Rob would then need an impressive new nickname to stay one step ahead of the library cops.

Finally, Yellowstone Rob would need to start speaking about Yellowstone Rob's self exclusively in the third person until Yellowstone Rob's new identity became second nature in Yellowstone Rob's mind.

Done, done, and done.

New York v. T— & Co.

Recently, the main character of *The Deal of the Art* returned in a gritty expose entitled, *People of the State of New York versus Donald J. T—, a Couple of His Sons, a Pair of Associates, and a Menagerie of Business Entities* (*New York v. T— & Co.* for short).

New York v. T— & Co. showcased Sixteen Frauds that helped propel the humble son of a slumlord from Queens to fame, fortune, and a stint in a corner office of an oval room at the pinnacle of Earth's mightiest nation.

Allegedly.

Fraud: A How-To Guide

Yellowstone Rob pored over the *New York v. T— & Co.* legal filings for tricks and tips that could allow any ordinary slob to represent himself as super wealthy, super quick, without any effort or natural talent. This was the masterclass that transformed Yellowstone Rob into The Wealthiest Person in Human History (On Paper)™.

Now Yellowstone Rob is on a mission to help others increase their own (On Paper)™ wealth, because it can't be called fraud if *everyone* does it.

Disclaimers

This book presents as "Frauds" the deceptive practices identified in the Complaint filed against T— & Co. by New York Attorney General Letitia James and confirmed as persistent fraud by New York Supreme Court Judge Arthur Engoron.

T— & Co. have denied all wrongdoing.

To illustrate the nature and effect of the Frauds, each has been taken to a logical extreme in the narrative of Yellowstone Rob's rise to become The Wealthiest Person in Human History (On Paper)™.

It should not be implied that T— & Co. would endorse Yellowstone Rob's financial misadventures.

T—'s name has been redacted while his case and its inevitable appeals are pending. Anyway, he's no one you would have probably heard of, and certainly not someone whose deep litigious pockets are continually topped off by small-money donors.

Still, it bears repeating that T— & Co. have denied all wrongdoing.

As you read this book, keep in mind that nothing in it is meant as actual business or legal advice. The Sixteen Frauds are presented for entertainment and educational purposes only. Deliberately misrepresenting (On Paper)™ or (Real World)™ assets or income to a financial institution, insurance company, business partner, or government entity could lead to civil or criminal liability.

Having said that, Yellowstone Rob must repeat that T— & Co. have denied all wrongdoing.

The Yellowstone Pledge

"I pledge to protect Yellowstone National Park. I will act responsibly and safely, set a good example for others, and share my love of the park and all the things that make it special."

The (Real World)™ Yellowstone National Park is a wonder of the natural world. Yellowstone Rob encourages everyone to enjoy the park responsibly.

Meanwhile, an entirely (On Paper)™ Yellowstone National Park forms an integral part of Yellowstone Rob's (On Paper)™ asset portfolio. Yellowstone Rob has provided this fictional depiction of the park for illustrative and entertainment purposes only.

Stay safe, my friends, and may all your frauds remain (On Paper)™!

The Civil Complaint

From the Trial of Donald J. T—

On September 21, 2022, New York Attorney General Letitia James brought a civil fraud case against Donald J. T—, Donald T— Jr., Eric T—, Allen W—, Jeffrey M—, The Donald T— Revocable Trust, The T— Organization, Inc., T— Organization, LLC, and associated properties and holdings ("T— & Co.").

Ivanka T—, an initial co-defendant, was dropped from the case on appeal, as her alleged frauds took place outside of the statute of limitations.

The Attorney General brought seven causes of action supported by evidence of sixteen deceptive strategies allegedly employed by T— & Co. between 2011 and 2021 to obtain loans and underwriting on preferential terms that could not be obtained otherwise.

In the complaint, the state attorney general identified $250 million of fraudulently obtained income derived by T— & Co. from transactions under New York jurisdiction. Additional transactions identified during an 11-week trial bumped that total to $370 million.

New York business law empowers the state attorney general to seek the disgorgement of ill-gotten gains she can prove in a court of law, the dissolution of business entities engaged in persistent fraud, and a ban on future business involvement of individuals proven to engage in persistent fraud.

Fraud #1

Claim to Own Everything

Including the value of partnership assets in which a person has only a limited interest with no control over disposition as if directly owned by them and under their control.

YELLOWSTONE NATIONAL PARK IS the crown jewel in Yellowstone Rob's (On Paper)™ real estate empire.

Since 1872, this unique and historic property has been held in a trust controlled by the American people (aka, The American People Limited Partnership Group). As a birthright member of the Partnership, Yellowstone Rob is a proud co-owner of every rock, tree, and dormant supervolcano within the boundaries of the 2.2 million-acre property.

Using Fraud #1, Yellowstone Rob can make an (On Paper)™ claim of ownership over the entire park.

The American People Limited Partnership Group controls many other parcels. All have their charms. But in his heart, in his soul, and in his (Papers)™, Yellowstone Rob only has (On Paper)™ designs on Yellowstone National Park.

To help his fellow Partnership members apply this Fraud for themselves, Yellowstone Rob has left the Partnership's non-Yellowstone assets on the table. These include scenic parklands, military bases, and landmark structures with impressive Greek Revival architecture. From practically anywhere in the United States, one or more of these Partnership assets is just a hop away!

All 330 million Partnership members are equally qualified to make non-exclusive, non-enforceable, (On Paper)™ claims to any of the Partnership properties. They are yours to enjoy, yours to protect, yours to pass down as a legacy to future generations, and yours to serve as the core of your (On Paper)™ development dreams.

The New York AG alleges that T— & Co. used Fraud #1 to misrepresent Donald T—'s control over cash assets between 2013 and 2021, escrowed assets between 2012 and 2021, and two properties owned by the Vornado Partnership (1290 Avenue of the Americas and 555 California Street) between 2011 and 2021.

(Real World)™ Opinion

Claiming (On Paper)™ ownership of a national park is harmless (On Paper)™ fun, but only as long as the claim remains (On Paper)™.

Making a (Real World)™ claim of exclusive ownership and control over a communal asset is an actual form of historical theft called "enclosure" because it was often done by enclosing the common land with a fence.

Enclosure is most famously described by the 17th Century English folk poem, "Stealing the Common from the Goose."

> The law locks up the man or woman
> Who steals the goose off the common
> But leaves the greater villain loose
> Who steals the common from the goose.

The law demands that we atone

When we take things we do not own

But leaves the lords and ladies fine

Who takes things that are yours and mine.

The poor and wretched don't escape

If they conspire the law to break;

This must be so but they endure

Those who conspire to make the law.

The law locks up the man or woman

Who steals the goose from off the common

And geese will still a common lack

Till they go and steal it back.

Over a span of centuries, the English enclosure movement fenced off much of the country's historically communal farmland and appropriated it for private use. This theft, no less audacious than Yellowstone Rob's claim, was justified by the Tragedy of the Commons theory.

According to the Tragedy of the Commons, if everyone were allowed to graze their animals in a common field, the grass and soil would be depleted, the land would become useless, and everyone would suffer. Much better for everyone, so the theory goes, if a single owner assumes the burden of preserving the land for its most profitable use.

Claiming ownership of partnership assets is another form of enclosure. This claim, made to a financial institution, is an implicit promise that if a loan defaults, the borrower can and will steal from business partners to pay off the debt. Or it may be claimed as an accounting error, and who can really be sure that it's not?

T— & Co. Examples

- One-third of the amount under "cash and cash equivalents" listed in T—'s 2018 financial statement belonged to Vornado Partnerships. Those are partnerships in which T— owns a minority 30% stake with no right to control distributions.

- In counting funds held in escrow, half of the amount listed under "escrow" in T—'s 2014 financial statement actually belonged to the Vornado Partnership.

Disclaimer

T— & Co. have denied all wrongdoing.

Fraud #2

Manifest a World without Limits (or Laws)

Valuing restricted properties subject to legal restrictions that negatively impact value as if they could be sold free and clear of such restrictions.

ASIDE FROM BEING ZONED as conservation land, Yellowstone National Park contains protected ecosystems, endangered species, historic structures, archaeological sites, mountains, lakes, gawking tourists, pesky park rangers, and other impediments to development.

Fortunately for Yellowstone Rob, Fraud #2 allows those pesky limitations of law and nature to just fall away.

2.2 million acres, at six single-family lots per acre, would yield 13.2 million (On Paper)™ homes. But let's call it 10 million, since Yellowstone Rob has set aside a nature preserve for endangered golfers in an area on the site plan labeled, "The Yellowstone Rob National Golf Club and Spa." This will be important to Frauds #13 through 15.

Yellowstone Rob has issued 10 million (On Paper)™ deeds through his imaginary (On Paper)™ Registry of Deeds in an act of safe and harmless (On Paper)™ fun.

The New York AG alleges that T— & Co. used Fraud #2 to misrepresent the legal restrictions on T— Park Avenue and Mar-a-Lago from 2011 through 2021 and on T— Aberdeen from 2014 through 2021.

(Real World)™ Opinion

Wealthy and powerful forces are tirelessly working toward a future where regulations don't exist or are only selectively enforced. The least scrupulous among them will push the boundaries by pretending their legislative victories have already been secured, that the pesky limitations of law don't apply to them, or that it's not illegal if you don't get caught.

T— & Co. have used Fraud #2 to load restrictions onto (Real World)™ properties to reduce (Real World)™ tax liabilities while carrying the unrestricted values on (Real World)™ financial statements. This type of (Real World)™ fraud shifts risk onto unwary lenders, distorts the financial marketplace, shifts tax liability from the developer onto other taxpayers, and unjustly enriches the fraudsters.

T— & Co. Examples

- In T—'s 2012 financial statement, rent-stabilized apartments at T— Park Avenue were valued as if they were unrestricted, leading to a nearly $50 million valuation for those units. An appraisal accounting for those units' stabilized status valued them collectively at just $750,000.

- The Mar-a-Lago club was valued as high as $739 million based on the false premise that it was unrestricted property and could be developed and sold for residential use. In reality, T— had signed deeds donating his residential development rights and sharply restricting changes to the property. Based on club-generated annual revenues of less than $25 million, the property should have been valued at closer to $75 million.

- The valuation for T—'s golf course in Aberdeen, Scotland,

assumed that 2,500 homes could be developed when the T— Organization had obtained zoning approval to develop less than 1,500 cottages and apartments, many of which were expressly identified as being only for short-term rental. The $267 million value attributed to those 2,500 homes accounted for more than 80% of the total $327 million valuation for the Aberdeen property on 2014 financial statements.

Disclaimer

T— & Co. have denied all wrongdoing.

Partial Summary Judgment

From the Trial of Donald J. T—

On September 26, 2023, Manhattan Supreme Court Justice Arthur Engoron issued a combined order on motions granting partial summary judgment in favor of the government, denying summary judgment to the defendants, and imposing sanctions on defendants and their attorneys.

The court granted partial summary judgment on the first of seven causes of action brought by the attorney general under New York State Executive Law § 63(12).

> Whenever any person shall engage in repeated fraudulent or illegal acts or otherwise demonstrate persistent fraud or illegality in the carrying on, conducting or

transaction of business, the attorney general may apply, in the name of the people of the state of New York, to the supreme court of the state of New York, on notice of five days, for an order enjoining the continuance of such business activity or of any fraudulent or illegal acts, directing restitution and damages and, in an appropriate case, cancelling any certificate filed under and by virtue of the provisions of section four hundred forty of the former penal law or section one hundred thirty of the general business law, and the court may award the relief applied for or so much thereof as it may deem proper.

The word "fraud" or "fraudulent" as used herein shall include any device, scheme or artifice to defraud and any deception, misrepresentation, concealment, suppression, false pretense, false promise or unconscionable contractual provisions.

The term "persistent fraud" or "illegality" as used herein shall include continuance or carrying on of any fraudulent or illegal act or conduct.

The term "repeated" as used herein shall include repetition of any separate and distinct fraudulent or illegal act, or conduct which affects more than one person.

Executive Law § 63(12)

The judge found that documents provided during the discovery phase satisfied the State's burden to establish, as a matter of law, that T— & Co. had overvalued assets and committed repeated and persistent fraud within the statute of limitations period from 2014 through 2021.

The Court invoked the Marx Brothers' movie "Duck Soup" to paraphrase T— & Co.'s arguments in their own defense as comparable to asking, "Well, who are you gonna believe, me or your own eyes?"

Fraud #3

Things Are Worth Whatever You Say

Valuing unsold apartments and homes at the offering plan or asking price rather than current market value.

WHAT'S A HOUSING LOT worth in Yellowstone Rob's (On Paper)™ housing community? One million dollars, no haggling. That's the number in Yellowstone Rob's offer brochures, which are so (On Paper)™, they're (On Glossy Stock)™!

Fraud #3 allows Rob to treat his asking price as an (On Paper)™ actual value. This Fraud and the previous two combine and stack like anime robots:

10 million unbuildable lots, each valued at one million because-Yellowstone-Rob-says-so dollars, on a parcel Rob can claim to own outright despite holding only a one-330-millionth share, equals $10 tril-

lion (On Paper)™. That's about 40 Elons of (On Paper)™ wealth already, as measured in January 2024 Elons according to *Forbes*.

With just three Frauds down and thirteen to go, Yellowstone Rob has already established himself as the Wealthiest Person in Human History (On Paper)™. The rest of the book will be gravy-flavored icing on a gravy-flavored cake.

The New York AG alleges that T— & Co. used Fraud #3 to misrepresent the value of units at T— Park Avenue from 2011 through 2015, at the Las Vegas Ruffin Joint Venture in 2017 and 2018, and at Mar-a-Lago in 2011 and 2012.

(Real World)™ Opinion

In a philosophical sense, value is always subjective. Even market value is based on subjective values applied through the mechanics of a market. Whenever a buyer and seller agree on a price, they add a data point to a set that can be used to establish the value of any similar item.

The data set is necessarily incomplete. Not every item has an asking price at any given time. Not every potential buyer is actively in the market. Not every assumption is necessarily correct.

The only thing we can be sure of is that price only correlates roughly with value. A sale price on canned beans doesn't make them any less desirable. The beans that sell for 20% more at one grocery store than another aren't 20% more delicious.

The New York Civil Fraud trial put a spotlight on the nature of real estate valuation. Every parcel is unique and every valuation is subjective, but standard methods within the industry should create values in a tight range that are as comparable and objective as possible. Any deviation from the standard methods should, at least, be disclosed to anyone who relies upon the resultant values to make a business decision.

In a footnote to the September 26, 2023, partial summary judgment order in *New York v. T— & Co.*, Justice Engoron suggested that an inflated price T— had justified as acceptable to a hypothetical "buyer from Saudi Arabia" might reflect influence peddling rather than savvy real estate investing.

Disclaimer

T— & Co. have denied all wrongdoing.

Fraud #4

Options Are Just Pre-Broken Promises

Valuing unsold apartments that are subject to a purchase option at a value far greater than the option price.

Yellowstone Rob is a man with options!

Options work like grocery store coupons to provide future discounts off future Yellowstone housing lots. Options are the stuff of unremembered dreams, uncollectable IOUs, and pre-broken promises. Rob distributes generous handfuls of options to family, friends, and business associates. They double as Christmas gifts. They are useful as napkins. Often, they once were napkins before being marked up with a Sharpie.

Are these options valid? Are they enforceable? Are they unregistered securities?

Those questions are entirely irrelevant to this book.

What matters is that Yellowstone Rob is using Fraud #4 to value all of his housing lots at the (On Paper)™ offer price, no matter how many units would likely sell at the steeply discounted option price.

Options make no impact to Rob's (On Paper)™ balance sheet but can be assets for others. Yellowstone Rob paid his lawyer in options, creating free money for both parties.

The New York AG alleges that T— & Co. used Fraud #4 to overvalue units at T— Park Avenue from 2011 through 2014.

(Real World)™ Opinion

Options, coupons, and gift certificates are assets. Their creation out of nothing is offset by an equal quantity of antimatter, which accountants refer to as liabilities. There's a good chance that an option will be shoved in a sock drawer and never used, but until it expires, its corresponding liability should be reflected somewhere on the balance sheet.

Disclaimer

T— & Co. have denied all wrongdoing.

Six Additional Causes

From the Trial of Donald J. T—

In partial summary judgment, the Court found persistent violations in the first of seven causes of action under New York Executive Law § 63(12) and ordered the cancellation of T— & Co.'s New York business certificates.

Six additional causes of action were to be brought to trial in three main areas: falsifying business records, falsifying financial statements, and insurance fraud.

Each defendant was the subject of an individual complaint for each action as well as conspiring jointly in a common scheme for each action.

Falsifying Business Records

Liability under New York Penal Law § 175.05 (falsifying business records in the second degree) requires that a person "[m]akes or causes a false entry in the business records of an enterprise."

Falsifying Financial Statements

Liability under New York Penal Law § 175.45 (issuing a false financial statement) requires that a person "represents in writing that a written instrument purporting to describe a person's financial condition or ability to pay as of a prior date is accurate with respect to such person's current financial condition or ability to pay, whereas [that person] knows it is materially inaccurate in that respect."

Insurance Fraud

Liability under New York Penal Law § 176.05 (insurance fraud) requires that a person submitted an application for insurance either: (1) knowing that it "contain[ed] materially false information concerning any fact material thereto"; or (2) "conceal[ed], for the purpose of misleading, information concerning any fact material thereto."

No Jury

These criminal statutes were, in this case, applied in a civil action seeking disgorgement of ill-gotten gains rather than jail time. The state had a lower burden of proof than in a criminal action in proving that the fraudulent statements were intentional and material to the transactions being questioned. A separate criminal case on any or all of these actions, and against any or all of these defendants, could still be brought by the Manhattan District Attorney.

As a civil action in equity in the State of New York, the 11-week trial was conducted by the judge without a jury.

Fraud #5

If You Can Dream It, You Can Earn It

Calculating net operating income with lower expenses and/or higher income than reflected in company financial statements.

FROM THE SALE OF options, Yellowstone Rob has funded an (In Metal)™ corporate headquarters in an (In Clearing)™ nook of his (On Paper)™ property.

The company has been optimized for quick relocations during park ranger patrols. And like the majestic Canada goose, corporate operations migrate south to avoid the frigid Montana winters.

The Yellowstone Rob Development Company has no actual (Off Paper)™ income, but with $10 trillion (On Paper)™ assets, thanks to previous Frauds, the billions are sure to start pouring in any day now.

Using Fraud #5, Yellowstone Rob can redefine reality, allowing whatever assumptions are required to reflect Rob's great expectations for the upcoming fiscal years.

Development services, management services, gift shop sales, and other potential income sources become creative entries in an (On Paper)™ spreadsheet, allowing Yellowstone Rob to represent the net operating income of a true (On Paper)™ whale.

The New York AG alleges that T— & Co. used Fraud #5 to inflate the net operating income of 40 Wall Street from 2011 through 2015, of Niketown from 2013 through 2020, of T— Tower from 2011 through 2014 and again from 2016 through 2019, and of two Vornado Partnership properties (1290 Avenue of the Americas and 555 California Street) from 2017 through 2021.

(Real World)™ Opinion

The income projections in a pitch deck are decorative at best. They're not presented as realistic, but as evidence that the business team has done the bare minimum of research and planning to provide a base level of confidence in the overall venture.

An accurate projection for Amazon, at the time of its founding, would have shown the company weathering a decade of consistent losses. Every business plan ever written has included a more profitable ten-year projection than Amazon's first ten years of actual profits, yet none of those other companies has gone on to match Amazon's success.

But there's a difference between a projection built on rosy assumptions and one built on lies, misrepresentations, and accounting tricks.

T— & Co. Example

- The net operating income for T— Tower relied in some instances on favorable numbers obtained by mixing time periods, using future income that exceeded the T— Organization's internal budget projections, and using expense figures that were lower than past expenses in audited financials.

Disclaimer

T— & Co. have denied all wrongdoing.

Fraud #6

Think Inside the Box

Using cherry-picked capitalization rates to derive the rates to use for valuations while ignoring higher rates listed for more comparable properties.

YELLOWSTONE ROB'S (ON PAPER)™ income statements show projected income from the development and sale of (As Yet On Paper)™ single-family homes.

Is it a problem that Yellowstone Rob has no experience building anything more complicated than a Lego Batmobile? Not at all! Rob just needs to find the right capitalization rate to determine what ten million homes should cost to build.

Fraud #6 allows Yellowstone Rob to use an unrealistically low capitalization rate.

For example, Rob could plug in the standard cost of a cardboard box-fort, scale up to the square footage of a three-bedroom split-level ranch, and send his projected profits through the projected cardboard roof!

The New York AG alleges that T— & Co. used Fraud #6 to inflate the net operating income of 40 Wall Street in 2015, of Niketown from 2013 through 2019, of T— Tower from 2011 through 2014 and again from 2016 through 2019, and of the Vornado Partnership properties (1290 Avenue of the Americas and 555 California Street) from 2017 through 2019.

(Real World)™ Opinion

Do you know what a capitalization rate is? Yellowstone Rob sure doesn't. He could have put in a week or two of research to find out, but it wouldn't have changed this section of the book and might have deprived Yellowstone Rob of the joy that is a cardboard village.

You aren't reading this book to learn advanced accounting principles and Yellowstone Roy isn't writing it as a cure for insomnia.

What matters about the capitalization rate is that it's a number that gets plugged into a spreadsheet to create a bunch of other numbers, and those numbers get represented to lenders as either good or bad.

Not every deception has to be as blatant as taking a Sharpie to the projected path of a hurricane to include a state that wasn't actually in any danger.

If someone intentionally tweaks a capitalization rate to turn their results from bad to good, from good to better, from high-risk to low-risk, or from rejection to acceptance, that's a material fraud.

T— & Co. Example

- Capitalization rates for T— Tower were derived by cherry-picking an unsupported figure from, or averaging the lowest two or three capitalization rates listed in, generic marketing reports and ignoring rates in those same reports for buildings that were closer and more comparable to T— Tower.

Disclaimer

T— & Co. have denied all wrongdoing.

Publisher's Interlude #1

by Cryptoversal

Continued from Publisher's Forward...

About two weeks after Cryptoversal Books turned down Yellowstone Rob's book proposal, I woke up in the middle of the night. For some reason, I'd been dreaming about trying to escape from an endless maze of cardboard rooms.

Something clattered against my apartment window.

I thought I must have imagined it, but as I was drifting back to sleep, the glass pane clattered again and I became aware of a steady clacking sound in the distance.

I snuck to the window and peeked out from the side. Under a streetlamp, a man with a bright orange hat and raggedy brown suit was clicking pebbles between his fingers from one hand to the other.

"Yellowstone Rob?" I opened the window and shouted down, "I've called the police! They're already on the way."

"Did you really?" he asked. "From here it looks like *somebody* cut your phone line."

"Here in the 21st Century, we use mobile phones. I don't even have a landline."

"No? Well, some kind of line got all cut up. You might want to use that fancy mobile phone to call your cable provider in the morning."

I rubbed at the early stages of a stress headache in my temples. "I'm still not publishing your book, Rob."

"That's cool. Yellowstone Rob will just be on his way then. But...would it be possible to borrow two shovels, a tarp, a box cutter, and some duct tape?"

"What?"

"Also, some advice? You shouldn't leave your car door unlocked. Anyone could pop the trunk and plant any old thing in there." He looked thoughtfully at the back end of my car. "Yellowstone Rob hopes you didn't really call the cops. That could get awkward."

"Seems that writing books and committing frauds aren't the full extent of your talents," I grumbled.

"Five minutes of your time, that's all I ask. And I've conveniently scheduled five nighttime minutes that you weren't using anyway!"

I pulled on a sweatshirt and jeans and raced down the stairs, past Yellowstone Rob, to the trunk of my car. Had he done something horrible, or was he only kidding around?

"Here." Yellowstone Rob dangled a pair of latex gloves. "You'll want to put these on before handling the body—"

"The *body*?" I didn't take the gloves. I didn't wait for any more explanation. I pressed the latch and the trunk popped open.

"The body of evidence detailing Donald T—'s frauds," Rob finished.

The inside of my trunk was crammed with thick manila folders crammed with reams of paper. "What is all this stuff?" I asked.

"Yellowstone Rob made you copies of all the financial records from the trial of *New York v. T— & Co.* If you review them, you'll see what a service it would be for someone to synthesize all this for the public."

I paged through one of the folders, which turned out to contain the printout from a single spreadsheet. "Now you're claiming to be a forensic accountant?"

"Me? Nah, Yellowstone Rob is just the Wealthiest Person in Human History (On Paper). Having money (On Paper) gives Yellowstone Rob a natural affinity for this stuff. What Rob does is a crude exaggeration of T—'s subtle art, but that's what makes it great. Concentrated fraud is more accessible and easier to understand, y'see? Would you rather read a trunkful of financial documents or a single thin manuscript with bullet-points and illustrations?"

I sighed. "That T— Civil Fraud case in New York really is heating up. It's been all over my feed but I don't have the context to go much beyond the headlines. Give me the manuscript. No promises, but I'll pass it around at our next acquisitions meeting."

"You made a wise choice." Yellowstone Rob presented me with a fresh copy of the manuscript, now professionally printed and no longer wrapped around a series of bricks.

"What was that thing you were saying about shovels and a tarp?"

"Oh, right." Rob pulled nervously at his jacket. "About that. Yellowstone Rob may have done something harsh and hasty, and it may have gone terribly wrong. Under the body of evidence is...the evidence of a body. We should bury him on a golf course. He would have loved that. But we don't have much time—Yellowstone Rob only has about an hour of lead time ahead of the Secret Service!"

Continued in Publisher's Interlude #2...

Fraud #7

Keep the Best Part for Yourself

Ignoring the impact of ground lease terms in valuing properties subject to a ground lease.

IN SOME PLACES, LAND is expensive and buildings are expendable. Like in the Yellowstone Rob's development, where the land is a national treasure and the buildings are cardboard box-forts pretending to be housing. A ground lease is what makes it possible for Yellowstone Rob to keep the most valuable part while a tenant pays rent to live in a crappy house.

It's like a campsite, but better than a campsite because Yellowstone Rob keeps the house at the end of the lease.

Fraud #7 allows Rob to include the value of ground lease houses as part of his own (On Paper)™ personal financial statement while the houses are still owned by a tenant, have yet to be built, or need to be rebuilt after being carried away by a flood.

Or by a bear.

Or by an overly assertive park ranger who claims it's "illegal" to build a home on so-called "public land."

The New York AG alleges that T— & Co. used Fraud #7 to inflate the stated value of 40 Wall Street from 2011 through 2017, of Niketown from 2011 through 2020, of T— National Golf Club: Philadelphia from 2011 through 2020, and of TNGC: Hudson Valley from 2011 through 2020.

(Real World)™ Opinion

At his core, Rob is a T— fanboy who gleefully takes his idol's methods to ridiculous extremes in a simplified scenario, but only (On Paper)™ where no real harm is done.

To illustrate Fraud #7, it was easiest for Rob to be the landlord of Yellowstone ground leases rather than the tenant, whereas T— used Fraud #7 as the leaseholder of the 40 Wall Street and Niketown properties. Ground lease terms are ignored in both cases, but Rob's misrepresentations inflate the value of the leased property while misrepresentations inflate the value of his leasehold interests.

T— & Co. Example

- T— is the holder of a ground lease at 40 Wall Street, a rented building on rented land. In valuing his leasehold interests, T— failed to account for relevant lease terms. Where a lender-ordered appraisal valued T—'s 40 Wall Street leasehold at $200 million in 2011, T—'s financial statement for that year listed a value of $524.7 million. This discrepancy was carried forward through 2018.

Disclaimer

T— & Co. have denied all wrongdoing.

Fraud #8

Everything is Comparable to Everything Else

Using sales of non-comparable properties to inflate valuations.

Hooray! Beautiful homes have been built on ground leases in Yellowstone Rob's burgeoning housing development. Take this beautiful four-bedroom colonial…

Seriously, take it off Yellowstone Rob's hands, please! A geyser erupted under the dining room and the structure is as soggy as yesterday's breakfast cereal. Now the bank is asking for an updated valuation! What's an (On Paper)™ real estate mogul to do?

Fraud #8 allows Yellowstone Rob to value a property by comparing it to a more valuable property and saying the two are, somehow, the same. Since all other properties are more valuable than this one, there can be no incorrect choice.

What's comparable to a pile of cardboard riding into the troposphere on a blast of boiling water? The closest comparable Yellowstone Rob could find is a $14 million mansion in California. Rob can claim the two homes are comparable because both feature a built-in sauna and steam room.

The New York AG alleges that T— & Co. used Fraud #8 to inflate the stated value of 40 Wall Street from 2016 through 2021, of T— Tower in 2015, of Seven Springs from 2011 through 2014, of the T— Triplex from 2012 through 2021, of Mar-a-Lago from 2011 through 2021, of T— Aberdeen from 2014 through 2018, and of T— National Golf Club: Briarcliff from 2013 through 2021.

(Real World)™ Opinion

All real estate is unique, all values are subjective, and everything of value is comparable in some way to everything else of value.

However, the game of business requires participants to agree that there's a "right way" and a "wrong way" to value property. When the "wrong way" causes money to move from one person's pocket to another's, there's probably something hinky going on.

Just because the rules are arbitrary doesn't mean you can break them.

T— & Co. Example

- In 2015, after the Crown Building at 730 Fifth Avenue sold for a then-record-setting price, due in part to existing development, usage, and undeveloped "air rights" available for additional floors. The Crown Building sale was the sole comparable T— & Co. used to value T— Tower, which included no "air rights" and had less favorable development and usage. Properties more comparable to T— Tower were ignored. The value of T— Tower on T—'s 2015 financial statements was 24.6% over the 2014 value, which was already 34.2% more than the 2013 value.

Disclaimer

T— & Co. have denied all wrongdoing.

Frivolous Motions
From the Trial of Donald J. T—

In the combined September 26, 2023, order, the Court invoked the Bill Murray movie "Groundhog Day" to describe the feeling upon rejecting the same arguments having previously been made over and over again by T— & Co.

Justice Engoron described the defendants as living in a "fantasy world" where:

- "rent-regulated apartments are worth the same as unregulated apartments;

- "restricted land is worth the same as unrestricted land; restrictions can evaporate into thin air;

- "a disclaimer by one party casting responsibility on another party exonerates the other party's lies;

- "the Attorney General of the State of New York does not have capacity to sue or standing to sue...under a statute expressly designed to provide that right;

- "all illegal acts are untimely if they stem from one untimely act; and

- "square footage [is] subjective."

As a result, five defense attorneys who should have known better were sanctioned $7,500 apiece for filing frivolous motions.

Fraud #9

Size Matters Not

Using an inflated square footage when pricing a property by the square foot.

THERE ARE TIMES WHEN size matters. For example, when Yellowstone Rob tells his story about the fish that got away. It was as big as Yellowstone Rob's outstretched arms after three rounds of surgical finger extensions!

The size of a property is just like that fish, like Yellowstone Rob's fingers, or like Donald T—'s frauds. Sometimes, things have to be stretched to create a more entertaining story.

Fraud #9 allows Yellowstone Rob to value a two-foot cardboard box as if it were a 2400-square-foot home. Maybe it's intentional fraud. Maybe it's an honest mistake. Maybe it's just a fish story. Math is hard, and who among us really understands how yardsticks, tape measures, and calculators work their measuring magic?

Come to think of it, who decided to measure lengths and areas using only human-sized feet? Some speciesist human supremacist from the unenlightened past, no doubt. Housecats, mice, and even insects have perfectly good feet, and more of them. Over on the metric system, technological advances have reduced the size of accelerometers, thermometers, and many other meters, so it only makes sense for square meters to keep up with the times.

For Yellowstone Rob, dimensional embellishments are worth the extra effort every time a child's eyes light up at the prospect of having a new bedroom, playroom, and media lounge. It's all in the box, kid, with plenty of space left over for an aquarium full of fish that got away!

The New York AG alleges that T— & Co. used Fraud #9 to inflate the stated value of the T— Triplex from 2012 through 2016.

(Real World)™ Opinion

If you're buying a house or renting an apartment, you should understand that value is measured by the square foot and that accuracy matters.

If you're a landlord, real estate agent, or developer, you should *definitely* understand that value is measured by the square foot and that accuracy matters.

If you are the patriarch of a real estate development dynasty with a lifetime of valuation experience, you should *definitely, definitely, definitely* understand that value is measured by the square foot and that accuracy matters.

T— & Co. Example

- T—'s triplex apartment in T— Tower was valued as being 30,000 square feet when it was actually 10,996 square feet. As a result, in 2015 the apartment was valued at $327 million in total, or $29,738 per square foot. At that point, only one apartment in New York City had ever sold for even $100 million, at a price per square foot of less than $10,000, and that sale was in a newly built, ultra-tall tower. In the

30-year-old T— Tower, the record sale as of 2015 was a mere $16.5 million at a price of less than $4,500 per square foot.

A discrepancy of this order of magnitude, by a real estate developer sizing up his own living space of decades, can only be considered fraud.

Justice Arthur Engoron, Sep. 26, 2023

Disclaimer

T— & Co. have denied all wrongdoing.

Fraud #10

Shift Future Profits into the Now

Failing to conduct a discounted cash-flow analysis to derive the present value of anticipated future income.

WANT A LIFE OF luxury that costs you nothing while burdening your descendants with the bill? Yellowstone Rob has taken Fraud #10 to its logical extreme, and is offering a free house for you that transforms into nondischargeable debt for your heirs!

Legitimate accountants will say the present value of anticipated future income should always be discounted. On the other hand, accountants using Fraud #10 will disagree, and aren't they also entitled to their opinion?

This type of conflict can only be settled in the marketplace of ideas and may take decades to resolve. Until then, Yellowstone Rob proposes that the Fraud side and the non-Fraud side should be equally respected.

Rob will admit that the fraudulent accountants are starting the battle as underdogs but don't count them out yet. The collective lobbying efforts of the real estate industry can't be underestimated.

If you take the deal, Yellowstone Rob's accountants will also enhance the value of your great-grandchildren's obligations by factoring in the added value you'll get by laughing at them from beyond the grave. Bonus!

The New York AG alleges that T— & Co. used Fraud #10 to inflate the stated value of Seven Springs from 2011 through 2014, of the Las Vegas Ruffin Joint Venture from 2013 through 2021, of T— Aberdeen from 2011 through 2018, of T— National Golf Club: Briarcliff from 2011 through 2021, of TNGC: LA from 2011 through 2021, of TNGC: Colts Neck in 2011, of TNGC: Philadelphia from 2011 through 2012, of TNGC: DC from 2011 through 2012, of TNGC: Charlotte in 2012, and of Licensing Development Fees from 2011 through 2018.

(Real World)™ Opinion

This is Economics 101. Or Finance 101. Or Accounting 101. When approaching issues of net profits, values, or cash flow from any angle, the concept of discounted future value will repeatedly pop up to smack you in the face and scream, "Today's dollar is worth more than tomorrow's dollar!"

Just ask any old person about their childhood and be prepared for the story about how they once bought out an entire candy store with a nickel—and got three cents back in change.

That's one of the reasons why cryptocurrencies seem so unnatural. In 2010, two large pizzas cost 10,000 bitcoins. At the start of 2024, 6 bitcoins could purchase an entire Domino's franchise. But even within the most artificially deflationary blockchain economy, getting paid today is still better than getting paid tomorrow.

Disclaimer

T— & Co. have denied all wrongdoing.

The Independent Monitor

From the Trial of Donald J. T—

As the Court found a propensity for T— & Co. to engage in persistent fraud, the Honorable Barbara S. Jones, a retired federal judge, was appointed to serve as an independent monitor until the case could be finalized. Jones would serve as an officer of the court within the T— Organization with access to its ongoing financial records.

Jones had served in the U.S. Department of Justice's Manhattan Strike Force Against Organized Crime and Racketeering, as an Assistant United States Attorney, and as an Assistant District Attorney for New York County.

She was appointed as a federal judge to the United States District Court for the Southern District of New York by Bill Clinton in 1995 and retired from the court in 2013 to go into private practice.

The scrutiny of Judge Jones was meant to deter further violations, but the violations continued:

> *[S]ince my appointment I have reviewed material financial and accounting information submitted by the Trump Organization. As part of my review, I have made preliminary observations regarding certain current financial disclosures with respect to the Trump Organization's reporting of financial information. Specifically, I have observed that information regarding certain material liabilities provided to lenders - such as intercompany loans between or among Trust entities and Donald J. Trump, certain of the Trust's contingent liabilities, as well as refundable golf club membership deposits-has been incomplete. The Trust also has not consistently provided all required annual and quarterly certifications attesting to the accuracy of certain financial statements.*
>
> *In addition, annual audited financial statements for certain entities, prepared by an external accounting firm, list depreciation expenses. However, interim internally prepared financial statements provided to third parties for these same entities inconsistently report depreciation expenses.*
>
> Hon. Barbara S. Jones (ret), Aug 3, 2023

Fraud #11

Be the Brand

Increasing the stated value of a property by a fixed percentage to reflect the value of your personal brand.

YELLOWSTONE ROB ISN'T JUST a person, he's a hair gel! He's a pair of designer shades! He's a pink puffy kerosene-soaked jacket! In short, he's a brand!

Just ask the bankers who fight over Yellowstone Rob-branded deals while ignoring all the ho-hum billionaires who *don't* license their likenesses for digital trading cards.

Actual wealth doesn't matter when you have a brand name. That's why Yellowstone Rob adds a 1000% premium to everything he owns. It's the only the most proper way to account for his being ten times awesomer than anybody else.

Just like the Midas Touch once enhanced values for a certain Cretan king, Fraud #11 allows Yellowstone Rob to tack an extra zero onto everything he touches as well.

The New York AG alleges that T— & Co. used Fraud #11 to inflate the stated value of Mar-a-Lago from 2011 through 2015, of T— National Golf Club: Jupiter from 2013 through 2020, of TNGC: LA from 2013 through 2020, of TNGC: Philadelphia from 2013 through 2020, of TNGC: DC from 2013 through 2020, of TNGC: Charlotte from 2013 through 2020, and of TNGC: Hudson Valley from 2013 through 2020.

(Real World)™ Opinion

Brand value and goodwill are genuine accounting concepts that have legitimate applications. The brand premium just needs to be based on reality and properly disclosed. Fortunately, Yellowstone Rob is always up-front about what he's doing.

Unlike some people...

[T— Statements of Financial Condition] "double dip," both purporting not to include a brand premium while simultaneously including one of 15% or 30%.

Justice Arthur Engoron, Sep. 26, 2023

By the way, those TNGC things are "T— National Golf Clubs," i.e., clubs that people can join if they want to play national-quality golf. When seeing properties referred to as national golf clubs, Yellowstone Rob always pictures a patriotic-themed bag of putters, drivers, woods, and irons.

Yellowstone Rob is half-convinced that someone is trying to deliberately confuse the issue.

T— & Co. Examples

- T— & Co. increased the value of golf courses to incorporate a "brand premium" despite expressly advising in financial statements that brand value was not included in the figures, and despite GAAP rules prohibiting the inclusion of internally generated intangible brand premiums.

- In 2013 financial statements, the value of T—'s golf course in Jupiter, Florida was inflated by fraudulently adding 30% for the T— "brand." Combining the inflation from using the fixed-asset approach with the 30% brand premium, T— claimed that a club he purchased for $5 million in 2012 was worth more than $62 million in 2013.

- T—'s financial statements included the same fraudulent 30% brand premium for six other golf clubs.

Disclaimer

T— & Co. have denied all wrongdoing.

Fraud #12

Speculative Deals are Done Deals

Including income from speculative "to be determined" deals despite representing that only signed and committed deals are included in a determination of value.

YELLOWSTONE ROB THINKS BULK mailing is the best marketing idea since drive-by megaphone trucks.

The mailing lists are cheap, postage is discounted, and every offer is a guaranteed (On Paper)™ sale. As they say at The Yellowstone Rob Development Company, the only non-customers are the mailing addresses that bounce back as undeliverable.

Fraud #12 allows Yellowstone Rob to value speculative deals (On Paper)™ as if they were done deals (On the Kind of Paper That

Forms a Legally Binding Contract)™. The more speculative the deal, the more done they should be considered.

Bonus tip: by printing bulk mail on non-biodegradable paper, Yellowstone Rob can declare a deal as pending even after the offer ends up in a landfill!

The New York AG alleges that T— & Co. used Fraud #12 to inflate the stated value of Licensing Development Fees from 2015 through 2018.

(Real World)™ Opinion

Somewhere in *The Deal of the Art*, probably, is advice about not counting chickens before they're hatched. This is very good advice.

Disclaimer

T— & Co. have denied all wrongdoing.

Publisher's Interlude #2

by Cryptoversal

Continued from Publisher's Interlude #1...

"Turn right here," I directed.

We drove past the Legs n' Buns Yoga Studio, past St. Mary's cemetery, over the train tracks, through a barb wire fence, and onto the overgrown grounds of the former army base. Night sounds encroached from the trees around us and the starry sky above.

"This is not a golf course," noted Yellowstone Rob. "Yellowstone Rob asked you to direct him to the nearest golf course."

"Not every mistake can be solved by burying a body on a golf course," I told him.

"He buried his ex-wife on a golf course," Rob countered. "A golf course in New Jersey! Yellowstone Rob isn't much of a golf person, but he had to stop by to see for himself. Only a year later, and the site was almost impossible to see. No landscaping, and weeds had overgrown the grave marker. Isn't that just the most perfect thing you've ever heard?"

"Maybe if you're a mob boss in *The Sopranos*."

It turned out that Yellowstone Rob was a fan of mob-themed media, and launched into a discussion of *Godfather* references in *The Sopranos*. I stayed silent. I used to publish magazines on a topic that led some unsavory folks to cutting themselves in for a piece of the action. I still had some trauma, but that was where I'd met my friend at the morgue, the one who could make bodies disappear forever, and I still had a favor to call in.

The road curved to run along the river. It wouldn't be long before it met up with another barb wire fence at the back of the hospital campus. Maybe someone would get a presidential kidney out of this mess. Certainly the corneas wouldn't go to waste.

I still was trying to convince myself that good outcomes could come from a bad situation when a dark shape blurred across our path. *The police? The army? The Secret Service?*

"Deer!" Yellowstone Rob swerved to avoid the animal, sending the car over the embankment. We tumbled, buffeted by airbag curtains and showered by shards of glass until the car splashed into the river.

Wheels down.

Roof up.

Wet feet, but not enough depth to swamp the car or carry it away.

The engine had died, but the windows still had power. I felt some painful spots that would become bruises, but no broken bones. No open wounds. No blood. Yellowstone Rob groaned but signaled with a thumbs-up that he was all right as well.

All in all, it was the best landing we could have hoped for, except for the part where my car was totaled in the middle of nowhere with a rather famous body in the trunk.

Continued in Publisher's Afterword...

Fraud #13

Make Their Values Your Values

Using a fixed assets approach to value a golf course.

T HERE'S MORE TO REAL estate than just land and buildings. There are also holes in the ground with tin cups and little flags sticking out of them. A patch of sand here, some grass over there, and those holes have just become a golf course. As long as you've counted the holes correctly.

But the Yellowstone Rob National Golf Club and Spa is more than just a dozen-and-a-half subterranean tin cans and the natural obstacles that surround them. It's also an accounting system to value those cans (On Paper)™ at an unreasonably high number.

Fraud #13 allows Yellowstone Rob to value his golf course based on its development costs rather than what a buyer might pay for it. For example, a course that winds around volcanic calderas and up a sheer cliffside would be among the most valuable in the world, due to its enormously high costs of development, despite being inaccessible, unplayable, and otherwise worthless.

The New York AG alleges that T— & Co. used Fraud #13 to inflate the stated value of T— Aberdeen from 2011 through 2021, of T— Turnberry from 2017 through 2021, of T— National Golf Club: Jupiter from 2013 through 2020, of TNGC: Briarcliff from 2012 through 2021, of TNGC: LA from 2013 through 2021, of TNGC: Colts Neck from 2012 through 2020, of TNGC: Philadelphia from 2011 through 2021, of TNGC: DC from 2013 through 2020, of TNGC: Charlotte from 2012 through 2020, and of TNGC: Hudson Valley from 2011 through 2021.

(Real World)™ Opinion

Not much to say about this one, but how weird is it that 17 holes on a plot of land are worthless while 18 holes on a plot of land can be worth a fortune? Serious golfer friends tell me it's because a six-pack of beer won't divide evenly into 17 holes of golf.

T— & Co. Examples

- An April 2014 appraisal valued the golf club portion of TNGC Briarcliff at $16,500,000; later that same year, Donald Trump valued the golf club portion of TNGC Briarcliff at $73,430,217, an inflation of more than 300%, in his Statement of Financial Condition.

- A 2015 appraisal valued the golf club portion of TNGC LA at $16,000,000 as of December 26, 2014; the 2015 Statement of Financial Condition valued the golf club portion of TNGC LA at $56,615,895, an inflation of more than 200%.

Disclaimer

T— & Co. have denied all wrongdoing.

Fraud #14

No Refunds (On Paper)™

Inflating the purchase price of a golf course by including membership deposit liability which itself is valued at zero.

THE YELLOWSTONE ROB NATIONAL Golf Course and Spa is set far away from tourists and park rangers on a patch of rocky terrain accessible only to mountain goats.

This location has given the club an air of exclusivity. However, since all current members are mountain goats, it's been difficult for Yellowstone Rob to collect membership dues.

Yellowstone Rob has offered club memberships for a $100,000 refundable deposit. That way, goats can golf all the golf that they can golf and still receive a full refund at any time. But every time Rob asks a goat whether it wants a refund, they always answer, "Naaaaaah!"

Fraud #14 allows Yellowstone Rob to count each mountain goat's refundable deposit as an (On Paper)™ asset of the golf club, raising the club's (On Paper)™ value accordingly. Because a goat asking for a refund would be inconceivable.

The New York AG alleges that T— & Co. used Fraud #14 to inflate the stated value of T— National Golf Club: Jupiter from 2013 through 2020, of TNGC: Colts Neck from 2011 through 2020, of TNGC: Philadelphia from 2011 through 2021, of TNGC: DC from 2013 through 2020, of TNGC: Charlotte from 2012 through 2020, and of TNGC: Hudson Valley from 2011 through 2021.

T— & Co. Example

- T—'s golf course in Jupiter, Florida was inappropriately valued using a fixed-asset approach with a purchase price that was inflated by the purported assumption of "refundable" membership liabilities. T— claimed to have paid $46 million for the club, consisting of $5 million in cash and $41 million in assumed membership liabilities. In financial statements, T— did not disclose the inclusion of those liabilities in the price of the club, stating that his potential liability for those membership deposits was zero.

Disclaimer

T— & Co. have denied all wrongdoing.

The Gag Order

From the Trial of Donald J. T—

During the trial, Donald T— posted, reposted, and amplified harassing and intimidating social media messages about Judge Engoron, and District Attorney Letitia James.

In statements before news cameras at the courthouse, T— questioned the merits and legitimacy of the proceedings, the motives of the prosecution, and what he perceived to be biases of the judge.

These statements were despicable, but legally protected free speech under the First Amendment.

The one restriction placed upon T— by the court was for him to refrain from attacking court staff, most notably including Judge Engoron's principal law clerk.

The limited gag order was imposed after T— attempted to implicate the clerk in alleged ethical violations, improper conduct, and a relationship with a prominent Democratic politician. These false allegations led to threats against the clerk from some of followers, causing the judge to place the gag order for the clerk's protection as judges are allowed to do.

T— violated the order twice, leading to the imposition of fines and the promise of increasingly severe punishments for further violations.

After a failed appeal to have the gag order removed, T—'s attorney cited it as the reason for canceling T—'s planned testimony in his own defense.

Fraud #15

Make Them Play Shoulder to Shoulder

Valuing unsold memberships at inflated prices.

Yellowstone Rob has never actually played golf, so he doesn't suffer from the problem of golf-playing course developers whose experience limits their imagination. Rob's golf inexperience is his super power, leading him to some truly magical innovations.

For example, Rob quickly identified wasted space as an inefficiency of traditional golf courses, where 18 holes might sprawl over 160 acres. With an average of 4 golfers on any given hole, that's a maximum of only 72 active players at a time. Rob's course crams those same 18 holes into a single acre, allowing 160 times as many members to enjoy the game.

The Yellowstone Rob National Golf Club and Spa has already attracted its first 72 mountain goat members, but Fraud #15 allows Yellowstone Rob to multiply that number by 160, the club's imagined capacity, and to assign an (On Paper)™ value to each of those unsold memberships.

The New York AG alleges that T— & Co. used Fraud #15 to inflate the net value of T— National Golf Club: Briarcliff in 2011, of TNGC: Colts Neck in 2011, of TNGC: Philadelphia from 2011 through 2012, of TNGC: DC from 2011 through 2012, of TNGC: Charlotte in 2012, and of TNGC: Hudson Valley from 2011 through 2012.

T— & Co. Example

- For T—'s golf course in Westchester, the valuation for 2011 assumed new members would pay an initiation fee of nearly $200,000 for each of the 67 unsold memberships, even though many new members in that year paid no initiation fee at all. In some instances, T— specifically directed club employees to reduce or eliminate the initiation fees to boost membership numbers.

Disclaimer

T— & Co. have denied all wrongdoing.

Fraud #16

Be Your Own Best Customer

Including fees from related party transactions as if they were negotiated transactions with outside entities.

T HE PREVIOUS FRAUDS HAVE left The Yellowstone Rob Development Company flush with (On Paper)™ profits. But many of those profits are being nibbled away by such (Off Paper)™ costs as legal, accounting, clerical, and janitorial expenses.

To streamline operations of The Yellowstone Rob Development Company, Yellowstone Rob founded The Yellowstone Rob Development Company Development Company, whose mission is to develop Yellowstone Rob development companies.

Fraud #16 allows the fees from one company to become the profits of an associated company, and vice versa, back and forth in a feedback loop of near-infinite (On Paper)™ profits.

For maximum efficiency, the two companies have established their corporate headquarters side-by-side on the same plot of Yellowstone land. As a side benefit, each company's overhead is now only half of what it had been before.

The New York AG alleges that T— & Co. used Fraud #16 to inflate the net value of Licensing Development Fees from 2013 through 2021.

T— & Co. Example

- In the category of "Real Estate Licensing Deals" on State-ments of Financial Conditions, values of deals between Trump Organization entities were improperly represented as being derived from "association with others," resulting in an overvaluation of up to $224 million in 2014, $110 million in 2015, $120 million in 2016, $113 million in 2017, $115 million in 2018, $97 million in 2020, and $106 million in 2021.

Disclaimer

T— & Co. have denied all wrongdoing.

The Worthless Clause

Don't Stand By Your Numbers

Including a legal disclaimer on fraudulent documents intended to shift all risk and liability from the perpetrator of fraud onto the victims of fraud.

THE WORTHLESS CLAUSE IS a bonus Fraud that wasn't listed in the Attorney General's Complaint. It was instead raised by T— & Co. as an affirmative defense.

Under the Worthless Theory, a bit of fine print puts victims of fraud on notice that any (On Paper)™ numbers in a loan application are inherently unreliable. The numbers don't match reality, and all responsibility for uncovering the true numbers is shifted from the loan applicant onto the suckers. I mean, onto the banks.

Assets are stated at their estimated current values and liabilities at their estimated current amounts using various valuation methods. Such valuation methods include, but are not limited to, the use of appraisals, capitalization of anticipated earnings, recent sales and offers, and estimates of current values as determined by Mr. Trump in conjunction with his associates and, in some instances, outside professionals. Considerable judgment is necessary to interpret market data and develop the related estimates of current value. Accordingly, the estimates presented herein are not necessarily indicative of the amount that could be realized upon the disposition of the assets or payment of the related liabilities. The use of different market assumptions and/or estimation methodologies may have a material effect on the estimated current value amounts.

T— "Worthless Clause"

Outside the courtroom, during the trial, T— elaborated on the theory:

"We have a clause in the contract, it's like a buyer beware clause. It says, 'When you take a look at the financial statement, don't believe anything you read' — this is up front. 'Don't believe anything you read.' Some people call it a 'worthless clause,' because it makes the statement, and anything you read in the statement, worthless. It says, 'Go out and do your own research, go out and do your own due diligence, you have to study the statement carefully. Do not believe anything.'"

Donald J. T—

Justice Engoron dismissed this theory. As he put it, "the 'worthless clause' does not say what defendants say it says, does not rise to the level of an enforceable disclaimer, and cannot be used to insulate fraud as to facts peculiarly within defendants' knowledge even vis-a-vis sophisticated recipients."

(Real World)™ Opinion

This Fraud attempts to nullify all other Frauds by reframing them as the terms of a contract. When your defense is that you told your victim that you were defrauding them as you were defrauding them, you probably don't have a very strong case.

However, the Worthless Clause is part of a long tradition of hidden terms inserted into boilerplate language that few people ever actually read.

For instance, this disclaimer was once used by Amazon Web Services to provide an escape clause in the event of a zombie apocalypse:

> *[T]his restriction will not apply in the event of the occurrence (certified by the United States Centers for Disease Control or successor body) of a widespread viral infection transmitted via bites or contact with bodily fluids that causes human corpses to reanimate and seek to consume living human flesh, blood, brain or nerve tissue and is likely to result in the fall of organized civilization.*
>
> AWS EULA 57.10 circa 2016

T— & Co. argued, at trial and in motions, that lenders didn't actually rely on the representations made in financial statements. The banks either knew or had cause to suspect that the numbers were exaggerated, but they wanted to associate their businesses with the prestige of his business, even if it meant assuming avoidable risks.

They argued that the misrepresentations were made out in the open by a person who is known to lie or exaggerate as part of his brand. These were worthless statements properly disclosed as worthless statements. And since the perpetrators of fraud usually hide what they are doing, this had to be something else.

Disclaimer

T— & Co. have denied all wrongdoing.

Conclusion

All Values are (On Paper)™ Values

Yellowstone Rob may be the world's first self-made (On Paper)™ trillionaire, but every billionaire, millionaire, and even most thousandaires store wealth in an (On Paper)™ realm where values are squishy and subjective.

Stock certificates are (On Paper)™. Real estate is valued (On Paper)™. Your bank balance is (On Paper)™. If you ask the bank for your money, you'll get an (On Paper)™ check. If you insist on cash, you'll get (On Paper)™ engravings of presidents.

And if you do get all your money totally (Off Paper)™ as gold or Bitcoin, you'll be punished and lose your ability to ever buy groceries again.

(On Paper)™ values aren't necessarily fraudulent. The fraud happens when (On Paper)™ values are misrepresented to induce others into losing some of their (On Paper)™ values.

T— & Co. didn't find themselves in a New York courtroom just because they used Frauds to pump their numbers, but because those pumped-up numbers were used to obtain loans and terms that would have been otherwise unavailable. The banks lost interest income, the marketplace was corrupted, and fewer lendable resources were made available to honest loan applicants for their needs.

American citizens possess a First Amendment right to lie about how much money they make and how much money they have. This right currently exists in political campaign speeches and on social media, but free-speech advocates are working tirelessly to extend the privilege to business records, loan applications, depositions, and trial testimony.

As a society, we must resist those efforts.

T— & Company deny all wrongdoing. However, the justice system, acting on behalf of our society, has the final word on what is or isn't fraud, and on how those frauds should be deterred and punished.

Publisher's Afterword

by Cryptoversal

Continued from Publisher's Interlude #2...

During our tumble into the river, Yellowstone Rob's orange hat had come off his head for the first time since I'd met him. He searched for it in the backseat while I climbed out through the passenger window and pulled myself onto the roof of the semi-submerged car.

The blinkers flashed, casting an on-again, off-again yellow glow onto the surface of the river.

Insects chirped in time with the clicking turn signal.

Trees rustled in the breeze.

From inside the trunk, something beat a panicked tattoo.

"Psst, Rob?" I hissed. "How sure are you about that body being dead?"

Yellowstone Rob popped his out the driver's side window. "Yellowstone Rob is the Wealthiest Person in Human History (On Paper)™. His opinions carry the (On Paper)™ weight of our entire (On Paper)™ capitalist system. When Yellowstone Rob declares someone (On Paper)™ dead, he expects them to stay (On Paper)™ dead."

"Yeah? Well, tell that to *him*."

The banging intensified, now accompanied by a muffled scream.

"This...is awkward," Rob admitted.

"I'll say. Someone is going to have to wait a long time for that presidential kidney." I jumped down into the chilly waist-deep water and waded across the rocky river bottom to the back of the car, my car, which had somehow become a watery crime scene.

I considered running away, making it on foot to an ATM, buying a burner phone, using underworld connections to obtain a new passport, and starting over in a country that doesn't extradite.

But who was I kidding?

At any moment, I expected Seal Team Six to drop from a black helicopter to rendition our asses to some facility that doesn't appear on any map.

Either way, my legacy would be as fodder for an *Unsolved Mysteries* episode. Or a true crimes podcast. Oh God, please don't let them make a true crimes podcast about me!

I opened the trunk.

Moonlight fell onto a body, wrapped in an expensive-looking suit and bloated like a days-old corpse. The face was discolored and a mat of straw seemed to have been stapled to the scalp, just as he'd so often looked when I'd seen him on TV.

"I've been treated unfairly. So unfairly. They're always treating me so unfairly," The man muttered to himself. He rolled from the trunk with a splash into the river.

I helped him back to his feet and tried to lead him to the riverbank, but he shook out of my grasp. He stood, adjusted his necktie, and flared his nostrils. "Who are you?"

"Me? I'm nobody."

"Yellowstone Rob also is nobody," called Yellowstone Rob. "Aw, nuts. Forget that Yellowstone Rob just said that. Aw, nuts again! Yellowstone Rob just realized how self-incriminating it can be to speak about Yellowstone Rob's self in the third person."

"That voice." The man from the trunk pointed an accusing finger at Yellowstone Rob. "The last thing I remember was that same voice, spoken by a man in an orange hat, a big man, a strong man, tears streaming down his face. 'Sir,' he said, 'sir, you've always been an inspiration to me. I've modeled my life after yours. I've modeled my frauds after yours. I've modeled my book after yours. Sir, you are my hero.' And that man was you!" He seemed to glow with rage, or maybe it was red from the tail lights.

"Did you really say all that?" I asked Yellowstone Rob.

"Not exactly." Rob dropped into the water to join us, orange hat in hand, to address the man from the trunk. "Sir, Yellowstone Rob was your true fan for decades. Yellowstone Rob read your book in high school, visited your tower in New York, and watched your business-themed reality game show. Yellowstone Rob even snuck into your Taj Mahal casino in Atlantic City to gawk at the opulent architecture. You were Yellowstone Rob's hero until more data points fell into a different pattern than Yellowstone Rob would have expected—your divisive and polarizing acts, the tower of lies built upon lies—and Yellowstone Rob had to accept that you were not the person you'd presented yourself to be. That includes the Sixteen Frauds from your trial."

"The Sixteen *Alleged* Frauds," the man stated.

"Alleged in (Real World)™ business communication, financial statements, and transactions," said Yellowstone Rob. "Alleged in a (Real World)™ trial with years of motion practice, months of testimony, and mountains of evidence."

"I've done nothing wrong!"

"And you may be vindicated by the courts," I assured him. "It could take years for all possible appeals to be exhausted. Until then, we promise to keep your full name out of Rob's book and make sure to emphasize that you and your associates deny all wrongdoing. Just please, please, please don't sue!"

"I offer a deal of the art." Yellowstone Rob extended a hand toward the man. "My book will present facts in good faith, sourced from publicly available legal filings in the New York Civil Fraud case. Illustrative examples will be presented as exaggerated flights of fantasy. Metatextual opinion will be embedded into an obviously fictionalized framing device depicting caricatures of the author, publisher, and primary subject."

"Plausible deniability," the man mused. "I won't be identified by name, so the book could be about *any* former president/businessman whose last name begins with T. Harry S. Truman, Lardbottom J. Taft, John F. Trennedy, George W. Tush..."

"The best part is that, as fictional caricatures, we wouldn't have to tie up any loose plot points," I added. "It won't matter that we're stranded in the middle of nowhere, facing possible assault and kidnapping charges, and I won't need to put in a claim for my car being totaled."

Deal?" asked Yellowstone Rob.

"Deal," said the man, and the two (On Paper)™ business tycoons sealed their (On Paper)™ arrangement with an (On Paper)™ handshake.

The End